Junket and Jumbles

You may consider poetry a serious subject,
but not all verse is serious, as is demonstra-
ted by this light-hearted collection. It is a
jamboree, a junket, a jumble of jokes and
jests, of rhymes, riddles, limericks and
tongue-twisters. How to judge what makes
people laugh is a difficult matter, but the
poems in this book can be said to have
children's 'seal of approval' – for all have
been tried and tested by young people and
found funny. Their sentence is to appear in
this anthology, for the delight and amuse-
ment of all its readers.

Junket & Jumbles

Raymond Wilson

Illustrated by Russell Coulson

Beaver Books

First published in 1977 by
The Hamlyn Publishing Group Limited
London · New York · Sydney · Toronto
Astronaut House, Feltham, Middlesex, England

© Copyright this collection
Raymond Wilson 1977
© Copyright Illustrations
The Hamlyn Publishing Group Limited 1977
ISBN 0 600 39161 2

Printed in England by
Cox and Wyman Limited
London, Reading and Fakenham
Set in Monotype Garamond

Contents

Acknowledgements

The author and publishers would like to thank the following people for giving permission to include in this anthology material which is their copyright. The publishers have made every effort to trace copyright holders. If we have inadvertently omitted to acknowledge anyone we should be most grateful if this could be brought to our attention for correction at the first opportunity.

George Allen & Unwin (Publishers) Limited for 'Voiceless it cries' from *The Hobbit* by J. R. R. Tolkien

Angus and Robertson Publishers for 'The Barber' by C. J. Dennis, from *A Book for Kids*

Nicholas Bentley for 'The Art of Biography' from *Clerihews Complete* by Edmund Clerihew Bentley

Blackie and Son Limited for 'Skippets, the Bad One' by Christine E. Bradley, from *Rhyme and Rhythm, Red Book*, published by Macmillan

Basil Blackwell Publisher for 'Momotara' by Rose Fyleman, from *Widdy-Widdy-Wurkey*

Chatto and Windus Limited for 'Cat' by Vernon Scannell, from *The Apple Raid*, a *Chatto Poets for the Young* book

William Collins Sons and Company Limited for 'The Visit' by Queenie Scott-Hopper, from *Junior Story Poems*

The Literary Trustees of Walter de la Mare, and The Society of Authors as their representative for 'Miss T' and 'Quack' by Walter de la Mare

Geoffrey Dearmer and The Society of Authors for 'Whale'

Andre Deutsch Limited for 'I have no voice and yet I speak to you' by John Cunliffe, from *Riddles, Rhymes and Rigmaroles*

Dennis Dobson Publishers for 'A thousand hairy savages', 'The Land of the Bumbley Boo', 'I'm not frightened of Pussy

Cats' and 'The Bongaloo' from *Silly Verse for Kids* by Spike Milligan

Gerald Duckworth and Company Limited for 'The Big Baboon' by Hilaire Belloc, from *Complete Verse of Hilaire Belloc*

E. P. Dutton for 'Jemima Jane' from *Around* and *About* by Marchette Chute. Copyright © 1957 by E. P. Dutton and reprinted with their permission.

Evans Brothers (Books) Limited for 'The Moon' by D. J. Enright, from *For Today and Tomorrow*; and 'Zoo Manners' by Eileen Mathias, from *Come Follow Me*

Faber and Faber Limited for 'And God Said to the Little Boy' and 'My Sister Clarissa Spits Twice' from *To Aylsham Fair* by George Barker; and 'The Rum Tum Tugger' and 'The Song of the Jellicles' from *Old Possum's Book of Practical Cats* by T. S. Eliot

Miss Elizabeth Fleming, William Collins Sons and Company Limited and the proprietors of *Punch* for 'In the Mirror' and 'The Cow' from *Gammon and Spinach*

Robert Graves and Cassell and Company for 'The Six Badgers' from *Collected Poems*

Vida Lindo Guiterman, sole owner of the following poems originally published by E. P. Dutton and Company: 'The Habits of the Hippopotamus' and 'On the Vanity of Earthly Greatness' from *Gaily the Troubador* by Arthur Guiterman

William Heinemann Limited for 'Mr Tom Narrow' from *The Wandering Moon* and 'The Bogus-Boo' from *More Prefabulous Animiles* by James Reeves

David Higham Associates Limited for 'Old Mrs Thing-um-e-Bob', 'Mr Pennycomequick' and 'I Saw a Jolly Hunter' by Charles Causley, from *Figgie Hobbin,* published by Macmillan

Houghton Mifflin Company for 'Grizzly Bear' by Mary Austin, from *The Children Sing in the Far West*

J. A. Lindon for 'Sink Song' from *Rhyme and Rhythm, Green Book,* published by Macmillan

J. B. Lippincott Company for 'The Reason for the Pelican', from *The Reason for the Pelican* by John Ciardi

Little, Brown and Company for 'Mrs Snipkin and Mrs Wobblechin' from *Tirra Lirra* by Laura E. Richards

The Longman Group Limited for 'Three Little Puffins' by Eleanor Farjeon, from *Lollipops*

Methuen Children's Books Limited for 'The King's Breakfast' and 'Happiness' by A. A. Milne, from *When We Were Very Young*; and 'Roundabout' by Clive Sansom, from *Dorset Village*

The Estate of the late Ogden Nash and J. M. Dent & Sons for 'The Tale of Custard the Dragon' by Ogden Nash

Oxford University Press for 'W' and 'Cows' by James Reeves, from *The Blackbird in the Lilac*

Jack Prelutsky for 'Toucannery' from *Lollipops* published by Longman

Richard Rieu for 'Dirge for a Bad Boy' by E. V. Rieu, from *The Flattered Flying Fish and Other Poems,* published by Methuen

The Society of Authors as the literary representative of the Estate of Rose Fyleman for 'Mice'

The Society of Authors as the literary representative of the Estate of A. E. Housman, and Jonathan Cape Limited, publishers of Laurence Housman's *A. E. H.* for 'The Grizzly Bear' by A. E. Housman

Mrs A. M. Walsh for 'Goldfish' by John Walsh

Happy thought

The world is so full of a number of things,
I'm sure we should all be as happy as kings.

Robert Louis Stevenson

W

The King sent for his wise men all
    To find a rhyme for W.
When they had thought a good long time
But could not think of a single rhyme,
    'I'm sorry,' said he, 'to trouble you.'

James Reeves

The king's breakfast

The King asked
The Queen, and
The Queen asked
The Dairymaid:
'Could we have some butter for
The Royal slice of bread?'
The Queen asked
The Dairymaid,
The Dairymaid
Said: 'Certainly,
I'll go and tell
The cow
Now
Before she goes to bed.'

The Dairymaid
She curtsied,
And went and told
The Alderney:
'Don't forget the butter for
The Royal slice of bread.'
The Alderney
Said sleepily:
'You'd better tell
His Majesty
That many people nowadays
Like marmalade
Instead.'

The Dairymaid
Said: 'Fancy!'
And went to
Her Majesty.
She curtsied to the Queen, and
She turned a little red:

'Excuse me,
Your Majesty,
For taking of
The liberty,
But marmalade is tasty, if
It's very
Thickly
Spread.'

The Queen said:
'Oh!'
And went to
His Majesty:
'Talking of the butter for
The Royal slice of bread,
Many people
Think that
Marmalade
Is nicer.
Would you like to try a little
Marmalade
Instead?'

The King said:
'Bother!'
And then he said:
'Oh, deary me!'
The King sobbed: 'Oh, deary me!'
And went back to bed.
'Nobody,'
He whimpered,
'Could call me
A fussy man;
I *only* want
A little bit
Of butter for
My bread!'

The Queen said:
'There, there!'
And went to
The Dairymaid.
The Dairymaid
Said: 'There, there!'
And went to the shed.
The cow said:
'There, there!
I didn't really
Mean it;
Here's milk for his porringer
And butter for his bread.'

The Queen took
The butter
And brought it to
His Majesty;
The King said:
'Butter, eh?'
And bounced out of bed.
'Nobody,' he said,
As he kissed her
Tenderly,
'Nobody,' he said,
As he slid down
The banisters,
'Nobody,
My darling,
Could call me
A fussy man—
BUT
I do like a little bit of butter to my bread!'

A. A. Milne

Grace

Heavenly Father bless us,
And keep us all alive;
There's ten of us for dinner
And not enough for five.

Anon.

School dinners

If you stay to school dinners
Better throw them aside;
A lot of kids didn't,
A lot of kids died.
The meat is made of iron,
The spuds are made of steel;
If that don't get you
The afters will.

Anon.

The story of Augustus
A boy who would *not* have soup

Augustus was a chubby lad;
Fat ruddy cheeks Augustus had;
And everybody saw with joy
The plump and hearty, healthy boy.
He ate and drank as he was told,
And never let his soup get cold.

But one day – one cold winter's day,
He screamed out –

                Take the soup away!
Oh, take the nasty soup away!
I *won't* have any soup today.

Next day begins his tale of woes;
Quite lank and lean Augustus grows.
Yet, though he feels so weak and ill,
The naughty fellow cries out still –
Not any soup for me, I say:
Oh, take the nasty soup away!
I *won't* have any soup today.

The third day comes: Oh what a sin!
To make himself so pale and thin.
Yet, when the soup is put on table,
He screams out loud as he is able –
Not any soup for me, I say:
Oh, take the nasty soup away!
I-won't-have-any-soup-today.

Look at him, now the fourth day's come!
He scarcely weighs a sugar-plum;
He's like a little bit of thread,
And on the fifth day, he was – dead!

Heinrich Hoffman

Manners

I eat my peas with honey,
I've done it all my life,
It makes the peas taste funny,
But it keeps 'em on the knife!

Anon.

The Goops

The Goops they lick their fingers,
   And the Goops they lick their knives;
They spill their broth on the tablecloth –
   Oh, they lead disgusting lives!
The Goops they talk while eating,
   And loud and fast they chew;
And that is why I'm glad that I
   Am not a Goop – are you?

Gelett Burgess

Greedy Jane

'Pudding *and* pie,'
Said Jane; 'O my!'
'Which would you rather?'
Said her father.
'Both,' cried Jane,
Quite bold and plain.

Anon.

There was a young lad of St Just
Who ate apple pie till he bust;
It wasn't the fru-it
That caused him to do it,
What finished him off was the crust.

Anon.

Miss T

It's a very odd thing –
  As odd as can be –
That whatever Miss T. eats
  Turns into Miss T.;
Porridge and apples,
  Mince, muffins, and mutton,
Jam, junket, jumbles –
  Not a rap, not a button
It matters; the moment
  They're out of her plate,
Though shared by Miss Butcher
  And sour Mr Bate;
Tiny and cheerful,
  And neat as can be,
Whatever Miss T. eats
  Turns into Miss T.

Walter de la Mare

The boy stood in the supper-room

The boy stood in the supper-room
Whence all but he had fled;
He'd eaten seven pots of jam
And he was gorged with bread.

'Oh, one more crust before I bust!'
He cried in accents wild;
He licked the plates, he sucked the spoons –
He was a vulgar child.

There came a burst of thunder-sound –
The boy – oh! where was he?
Ask of the maid who mopped him up,
The bread-crumbs and the tea!

Anon.

A cannibal bold of Penzance
Ate an uncle and two of his aunts,
A cow and her calf,
An ox and a half –
And now he can't button his pants.

Anon.

A thousand hairy savages
A thousand hairy savages
Sitting down to lunch
Gobble gobble glup glup
Munch munch munch.

Spike Milligan

If *a cannibal can nibble*

How many cans can a cannibal nibble
If a cannibal can nibble cans?
As many cans as a cannibal can nibble
If a cannibal can nibble cans.

Anon.

The old woman

There was an old woman who swallowed a fly;
I wonder why
She swallowed a fly.
Poor old woman, she's sure to die.

There was an old woman who swallowed a spider,
That went oops-oops right down inside her;
She swallowed the spider to catch the fly,
I wonder why
She swallowed a fly.
Poor old woman, she's sure to die.

There was an old woman who swallowed a bird;
How absurd
To swallow a bird.
She swallowed the bird to catch the spider
That went oops-oops right down inside her;
She swallowed the spider to catch the fly,
I wonder why
She swallowed a fly.
Poor old woman, she's sure to die.

There was an old woman who swallowed a cat;
Fancy that!
She swallowed a cat.
She swallowed the cat to catch the bird,
She swallowed the bird to catch the spider
That went oops-oops right down inside her;
She swallowed the spider to catch the fly,
I wonder why
She swallowed a fly.
Poor old woman, she's sure to die.

There was an old woman who swallowed a dog;
She went the whole hog
And swallowed a dog.

She swallowed the dog to catch the cat,
She swallowed the cat to catch the bird,
She swallowed the bird to catch the spider
That went oops-oops right down inside her;
She swallowed the spider to catch the fly,
I wonder why
She swallowed a fly.
Poor old woman, she's sure to die.

There was an old woman who swallowed a cow;
I wonder how
She swallowed a cow.
She swallowed the cow to catch the dog,
She swallowed the dog to catch the cat,
She swallowed the cat to catch the bird,
She swallowed the bird to catch the spider
That went oops-oops right down inside her;
She swallowed the spider to catch the fly,
I wonder why
She swallowed a fly.
Poor old woman, she's sure to die.

There was an old woman who swallowed a horse;
She died, of course!

Anon.

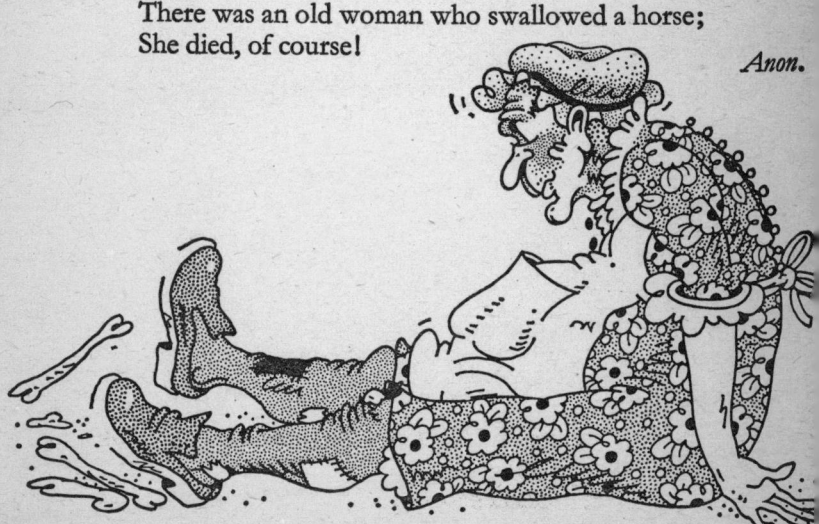

The deaf old woman

Old woman, old woman, will you go a-shearin'?
Speak a little louder, sir, I'm very hard of hearin'.

Old woman, old woman, will you go a-gleanin'?
Speak a little louder, I cannot tell the meanin'.

Old woman, old woman, will you go a-walkin'?
Speak a little louder, sir, or what's the use of talkin'!

Old woman, old woman, shall I kiss thee dearly?
Thank you, kind sir, I hear you very clearly!

Anon.

'Fire, fire!'

'Fire, fire!'
Said Mrs McGuire.
'Where, where?'
Said Mrs Ware.
'Down town,'
Said Mrs Brown.
'Heaven save us!'
Said Mrs Davis.

Anon.

There was a young lady of Riga
Who went for a ride on a tiger;
     They returned from the ride
     With the lady inside,
And a smile on the face of the tiger.

Anon.

Old Mrs Thing-um-e-bob

Old Mrs Thing-um-e-bob,
  Lives at you-know-where,
Dropped her what-you-may-call-it down
  The well of the kitchen stair.

'Gracious me!' said Thing-um-e-bob,
  'This don't look too bright.
I'll ask old Mr What's-his-name
  To try and put it right.'

Along came Mr What's-his-name,
  He said, 'You've broke the lot!
I'll have to see what I can do
  With some of the you-know-what.'

So he gave the what-you-may-call-it a pit
  And he gave it a bit of a pat,
And he put it all together again
  With a little of this and that.

And he gave the what-you-may-call-it a dib
  And he gave it a dab as well
When all of a sudden he heard a note
  As clear as any bell.

'It's as good as new!' cried What's-his-name.
  'But please remember, now,
In future Mrs Thing-um-e-bob
  You'll have to go you-know-how.'

Charles Causley

Mrs Snipkin and Mrs Wobblechin

Skinny Mrs Snipkin,
With her little pipkin,
Sat by the fireside a-warming of her toes.
Fat Mrs Wobblechin,
With her little doublechin,
Sat by the window a-cooling of her nose.

Says this one to that one,
'Oh! you silly fat one,
Will you shut the window down? You're freezing me to death!'
Says that one to t'other one,
'Good gracious, how you bother one!
There isn't air enough for me to draw my precious breath!'

Skinny Mrs Snipkin,
Took her little pipkin,
Threw it straight across the room as hard as she could throw;
Hit Mrs Wobblechin
On her little doublechin,
And out of the window a-tumble she did go.

Laura E. Richards

There was an old person of Tring
Who, when somebody asked her to sing,
Replied, 'Ain't it odd?
I can never tell *God
Save the Weasel* from *Pop Goes the King*!'

Anon.

Mr Tom Narrow

A scandalous man
  Was Mr Tom Narrow,
He pushed his grandmother
  Round in a barrow.
And he called out loud
  As he rang his bell,
'Grannies to sell!
  Old grannies to sell!'

The neighbours said,
  As he passed them by,
'This poor old lady
  We will not buy.
He surely must be
  A mischievous man
To try for to sell
  His own dear Gran!'

'Besides,' said another,
  'If you ask me,
She'd be very small use
  That I can see.'
'You're right,' said a third,
  'And no mistake –
A very poor bargain
  She'd surely make.'

So Mr Tom Narrow,
  He scratched his head,
And he sent his grandmother
  Back to bed;
And he rang his bell
  Through all the town
Till he sold his barrow
  For half a crown.

James Reeves

31

Get up and bar the door

It fell about the Martinmas time,
    And a gay time it was then,
When our goodwife got puddings to make,
    And she's boiled them in the pan.

The wind so cold blew south and north,
    And blew into the floor;
Quoth our goodman to our goodwife,
    'Get up and bar the door.'

'My hand is in my household work,
    Goodman, as ye may see;
And it will not be barred for a hundred years,
    If it's to be barred by me!'

They made a pact between them both,
    They made it firm and sure,
That whosoe'er should speak the first,
    Should rise and bar the door.

Then by there came two gentlemen,
    At twelve o'clock at night,
And they could see neither house nor hall,
    Nor coal nor candlelight.

'Now whether is this a rich man's house,
    Or whether is it a poor?'
But never a word would one of them speak,
    For barring of the door.

The guests they ate the white puddings,
    And then they ate the black;
Tho' much the goodwife thought to herself,
    Yet never a word she spake.

Then said one stranger to the other,
   'Here, man, take ye my knife;
Do ye take off the old man's beard,
   And I'll kiss the goodwife.'

'There's no hot water to scrape it off,
   And what shall we do then?'
'Then why not use the pudding broth,
   That boils into the pan?'

O up then started our goodman,
   An angry man was he;
'Will ye kiss my wife before my eyes!
   And with pudding broth scald me!'

Then up and started our goodwife,
   Gave three skips on the floor:
'Goodman, you've spoken the very first word!
   Get up and bar the door!'

Anon.

Man and wife

Jack Sprat would eat no fat,
His wife would eat no lean,
And so between the two of them
They kept the platter clean.
Jack ate all the lean,
Joan ate all the fat,
The bone they picked it clean
And gave it to the cat.

Jack Sprat was wheeling
His wife by the ditch,
The barrow turned over
And in she did pitch;
Says Jack, 'She'll be drowned,'
But Joan did reply,
'I don't think I shall,
For the ditch is quite dry.'

Anon.

There was an old man of Calcutta
Who spoke with a terrible stutter.
At breakfast he said,
'Give me b-b-b-bread,
and b-b-b-b-b-b-butter.'

Anon.

The man who wasn't there

As I was going up the stair
I met a man who wasn't there.
He wasn't there again today –
Oh, how I wish he'd go away!

Anon.

About chaps

The Art of Biography
Is different from Geography.
Geography is about Maps,
But Biography is about Chaps.

Edmund Clerihew Bentley

Boniface

Old Boniface he loved good cheer,
  And took his glass of Burton,
And when the nights grew sultry hot
  He slept without a shirt on.

Anon.

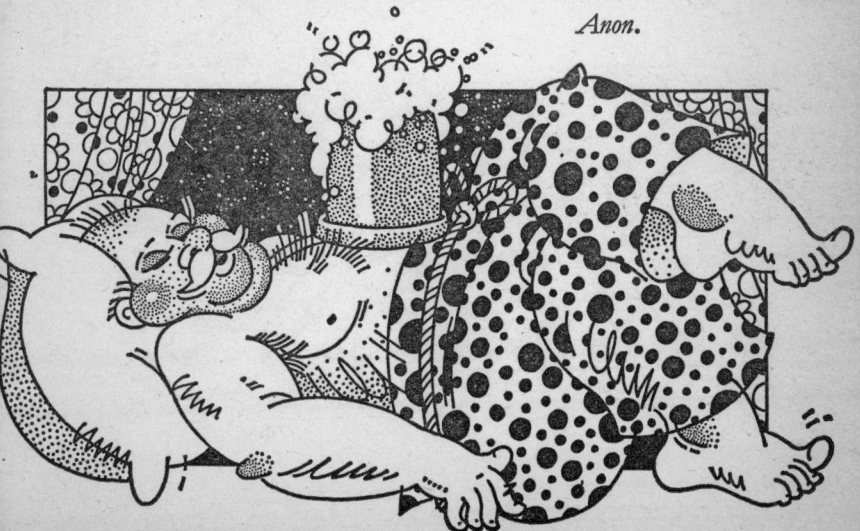

There was an old miser at Reading,
Had a house, and a yard with a shed in;
    'Twas meant for a cow,
    But so small, that I vow
The poor creature could scarce get her head in.

Anon.

Chewing his beard
On Nevski Bridge a Russian stood
Chewing his beard for lack of food.
Said he, 'It's tough this stuff to eat,
But a darn sight better than shredded wheat!'

Anon.

There was an Old Man with a beard,
Who said, 'It is just as I feared! –
    Two owls and a hen,
    Four larks and a wren,
Have all built their nests in my beard!'

Anon.

Michael Finnigin

There was an old man called Michael Finnigin
    He grew whiskers on his chin-i-gin,
The wind blew them out and the wind blew them in-i-gin,
    Poor old Michael Finnigin,
Begin-i-gin . . .

Anon.

The barber

I'd like to be a barber and learn to shave and clip,
Calling out, 'Next, please!' and pocketing my tip.
All day you'd hear my scissors going, 'Snip, Snip, Snip!'
I'd lather people's faces, and their noses I would grip
While I shaved most carefully along the upper lip.
      But I wouldn't be a barber if . . .
        The razor was to slip.
        Would you?

C. J. Dennis

Doctor Emmanuel

Doctor Emmanuel Harrison-Hyde
Has a very big head with brains inside.
I wonder what happens inside the brains
That Doctor Emmanuel's head contains.

James Reeves

Doctor Bell

Doctor Bell fell down the well
And broke his collar-bone.
Doctors should attend the sick
And leave the well alone.

Anon.

Doctor Foster

Doctor Foster went to Glo'ster
    In a shower of rain;
He stepped in a puddle up to his middle,
    And wouldn't go there again.

Anon.

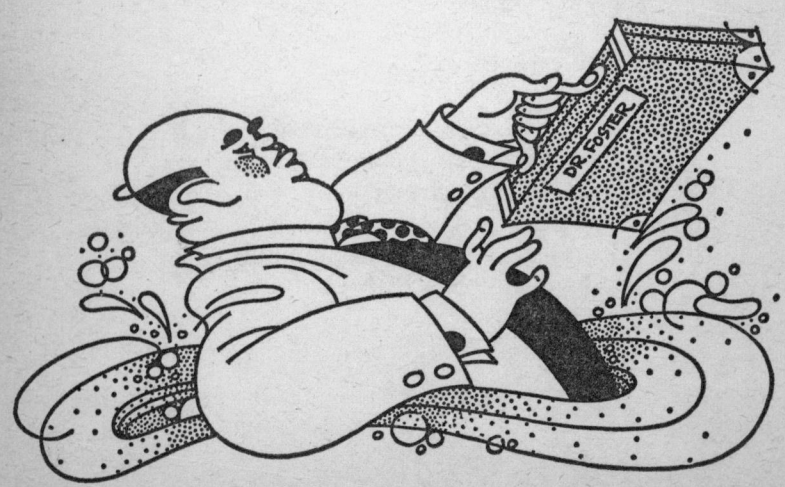

A tragic story

There lived a sage in days of yore,
And he a handsome pigtail wore:
But wondered much and sorrowed more
  Because it hung behind him.

He mused upon this curious case,
And swore he'd change the pigtail's place,
And have it hanging at his face,
  Not dangling there behind him.

Says he, 'The mystery I've found –
I'll turn me round' – he turned him round;
  But still it hung behind him.

Then round, and round, and out and in,
All day the puzzled sage did spin;
In vain – it mattered not a pin –
  The pigtail hung behind him.

And right and left, and round about,
And up and down, and in and out,
He turned; but still the pigtail stout
  Hung steadily behind him.

And though his efforts never slack,
And though he twist, and twirl, and tack,
Alas! still faithful to his back,
  The pigtail hangs behind him.

W. M. Thackeray

Bones

Said Mr Smith, 'I really cannot
    Tell you, Dr Jones –
The most peculiar pain I'm in –
    I think it's in my *bones*.'

Said Dr Jones, 'Oh, Mr Smith,
    That's nothing. Without doubt
We have a simple cure for that;
    It is to take them out.'

He laid forthwith poor Mr Smith
    Close-clamped upon the table,
And, cold as stone, took out his bones
    As fast as he was able.

And Smith said, 'Thank you, thank you, *thank* you.'
    And wished him a Good-day;
As with his parcel 'neath his arm
    He slowly moved away.

Walter de la Mare

I saw a jolly hunter

I saw a jolly hunter
  With a jolly gun
Walking in the country
  In the jolly sun.

In the jolly meadow
  Sat a jolly hare.
Saw the jolly hunter.
  Took jolly care.

Hunter jolly eager –
  Sight of jolly prey.
Forgot gun pointing
  Wrong jolly way.

Jolly hunter jolly head
  Over heels gone.
Jolly old safety-catch
  Not jolly on.

Bang went the jolly gun.
  Hunter jolly dead.
Jolly hare got clean away.
  Jolly good, I said.

Charles Causley

A grenadier

Who comes here?
  A grenadier.
What do you want?
  A pot of beer.
Where's your money?
  I've forgot.
Then get you gone
  You drunken sot!
Anon.

Daddy fell into the pond

Everyone grumbled. The sky was grey.
We had nothing to do and nothing to say.
We were nearing the end of a dismal day,
And there seemed to be nothing beyond,

THEN

Daddy fell into the pond!

And everyone's face grew merry and bright,
And Timothy danced for sheer delight.
'Give me the camera, quick, oh quick!
He's crawling out of the duckweed.' *Click!*

Then the gardener suddenly slapped his knee,
And he doubled up, shaking silently,
And the ducks all quacked as if they were daft
And it sounded as if the old drake laughed.

O, there wasn't a thing that didn't respond

WHEN

Daddy fell into the pond!

Alfred Noyes

42

The little elf-man

I met a little elf-man once
Down where the lilies blow.
I asked him why he was so small,
And why he didn't grow.

He slightly frowned, and with his eye
He looked me through and through —
'I'm just as big for me,' said he,
'As you are big for you!'

J. K. Bangs

To steal he stole

Forth from his den to steal he stole,
His bags of chink he chunk,
And many a wicked smile he smole,
And many a wink he wunk.

Anon.

There was a young fellow of Ceuta
Who rode into church on his scooter;
He knocked down the Dean
And said: 'Sorry old bean,
I ought to have sounded my hooter.'

Anon.

There was a young man of Devizes
Whose ears were of different sizes;
The one that was small
Was no use at all,
But the other won several prizes.

Anon.

Mr Pennycomequick

Mr Hector Pennycomequick
   Stood on the castle keep,
Opened up a carriage-umbrella
   And took a mighty leap.

'Hooray!' cried Mr Pennycomequick
   As he went through the air.
'I've always wanted to go like this
   From here to Newport Square.'

But Mr Hector Pennycomequick
   He never did float nor fly.
He landed in an ivy-bush
   His legs up in the sky.

Mr Hector Pennycomequick
   They hurried home to bed
With a bump the size of a seagull's egg
   On the top of his head.

'So sorry,' said Mr Pennycomequick,
   'For causing all this fuss.
When next I go to Newport Square
   I think I'll take the bus.'

The moral of this little tale
   Is difficult to refute:
A carriage-umbrella's a carriage-umbrella
   And not a parachute.

Charles Causley

Eaper Weaper

Eaper Weaper, chimbley sweeper,
Had a wife but couldn't keep her;
Had anovver, didn't love her,
Up the chimbley he did shove her.

Anon.

There was a young student of Crete,
Who stood on his head in the street,
Said he, 'It is clear
If I mean to stop here
I shall have to shake hands with my feet.'

Anon.

There was a young man of Bengal
Who went to a fancy-dress ball.
He went just for fun
Dressed up as a bun,
And a dog ate him up in the hall.

Anon.

Dirge for a bad boy

Richard has been sent to bed:
Let a solemn dirge be said.
Sent to bed before his time,
Sentenced for a nursery crime.
Draw down the blinds in every room
And fill the dismal house with gloom.
Richard has been sent to bed:
Let a solemn dirge be said.

Tell the cat and kitten they
Must cease from their unseemly play.
Stop the telephone from ringing;
Stop the kettle from its singing.
And hark, is that the hoover's hum?
Let the hoover too be dumb.
Richard has been sent to bed:
Let a solemn dirge be said.

Turn off, turn off, the central heat,
And let the cold creep round our feet.
Put out the fire and let it die
Underneath that juicy pie,
That we may eat (if eat we must)
Cold apple and a colder crust.
Richard has been sent to bed:
Let a solemn dirge be said.

And when the time has come for all
To follow through the darkened hall,
Let every sound of mirth be banned –
Take each a candle in his hand,
And winding up the stairway slow
In melancholy order go,
While this solemn dirge is said
For a poor sinner in his bed.

E. V. Rieu

Little Johnny

Little Johnny fished all day,
Fishes would not come his way.
'Had enough of this,' said he,
'I'll be going home to tea!'

When the fishes saw him go,
Up they came all in a row;
Jumped about and laughed with glee,
Shouting, 'Johnny's gone to tea!'

Anon.

Nobody cares

Tom tied a kettle to the tail of a cat,
Jill put a stone in the blind man's hat,
Bob threw his grandmother down the stairs –
And they all grew up ugly, and nobody cares.

Anon.

Please try

I wish you'd speak when you're spoken to,
I wish you'd do as you're bid,
I wish you'd shut the door after you,
I wish you'd be a good kid!

Anon.

A choice

There's lots of ways of doing things,
As every one supposes,
For some turn up their sleeves at work
And some turn up their noses.

Anon.

Happiness

John had
Great Big
Waterproof
Boots on;
John had a
Great Big
Waterproof
Hat;
John had a
Great Big
Waterproof
Mackintosh –
And that
(said John)
Is
That.

A. A. Milne

Godfrey Gordon Gustavus Gore

Godfrey Gordon Gustavus Gore –
No doubt you have heard that name before –
Was a boy who never would shut a door!

The wind might whistle, the wind might roar,
And teeth be aching and throats be sore,
But still he never would shut the door.

His father would beg, his mother implore,
'Godfrey Gordon Gustavus Gore,
We really do wish you would shut the door!'

Their hands they wrung, their hair they tore;
But Godfrey Gordon Gustavus Gore
Was as deaf as the buoy out at the Nore.

When he walked forth the folks would roar,
'Godfrey Gordon Gustavus Gore,
Why don't you think to shut the door?'

They rigged out a shutter with sail and oar,
And threatened to pack off Gustavus Gore
On a voyage of penance to Singapore.

But he begged for mercy, and said, 'No more!
Pray do not send me to Singapore
On a shutter, and then I will shut the door!'

Anon.

The rain

The rain it raineth every day,
   Upon the just and unjust fellow,
But more upon the just, because
   The unjust hath the just's umbrella.

Anon.

Brother Jim

An accident happened to my brother Jim
When somebody threw a tomato at him –
Tomatoes are juicy and don't hurt the skin,
But this one was specially packed in a tin.

Anon.

Momotara

Where did Momotara go,
With a hoity-toity-tighty?
He went to lay the giants low,
The wicked ones and mighty.

What did Momotara take?
His monkey, dog and pheasant,
Some dumplings and an almond cake,
Which made the journey pleasant.

How did Momotara fare
Upon the fearful meeting?
He seized the giants by the hair
And gave them all a beating.

What did Momotara bring?
Oh, more than you could measure:
A silver coat, a golden ring
And a waggon-load of treasure.

What did Momotara do?
He sat himself astride it;
The monkey pushed, the pheasant drew
And the little dog ran beside it.

Japanese nursery rhyme translated by Rose Fyleman

Speak roughly to your little boy

Speak roughly to your little boy,
    And beat him when he sneezes:
He only does it to annoy,
    Because he knows it teases.

Anon.

Peter Piper

Peter Piper picked a peck of pickled pepper;
A peck of pickled pepper Peter Piper picked.
If Peter Piper picked a peck of pickled pepper,
Where's the peck of pickled pepper Peter Piper picked?

Anon.

And God said to the little boy

And God said to the little boy
As the little boy came out of chapel
Little boy, little boy, little boy
Did you eat that there apple?
And the little boy answered No, Lord.

And God said to the little girl
As the little girl came out of chapel
Little girl, little girl, little girl,
Did you eat that there apple?
And the little girl answered No, Lord.

Then the Lord pointed with his finger
And fixed them both with his stare,
And he said in a voice like a Rolls Royce
Well, what are them two cores doing there?

George Barker

There was a young lady of Spain,
Who wouldn't go out in the rain,
  'Cause she'd lent her umbrella
  To Queen Isabella,
Who never returned it again.

Anon.

The visit

Amy Elizabeth Ermyntrude Annie
Went to the country to visit her Grannie;

Learnt to churn butter and learnt to make cheese,
Learnt to milk cows and take honey from bees;

Learnt to spice rose-leaves and learnt to cure ham,
Learnt to make cider and black-currant jam.

When she came home she could not settle down –
Said there was nothing to do in the town;

Nothing to do there and nothing to see:
Life was all shopping and afternoon tea!

Amy Elizabeth Ermyntrude Annie
Ran away back to the country and Grannie.

Queenie Scott-Hopper

Tables

Gertie Gables learnt her tables
Though it took her long.
Every night she got them right
Next day she got them wrong.

Anon.

Build a bonfire

Build a bonfire, build a bonfire,
Put the teachers on the top;
Put the prefects in the middle,
And we'll burn the blooming lot.

Anon.

Whatever the weather

Whether the weather be fine, or whether the weather be not,
Whether the weather be cold, or whether the weather be hot,
We'll weather the weather, whatever the weather,
Whether we like it or not.

Anon.

Jemima Jane

Jemima Jane,
　Oh, Jemima Jane,
She loved to go out
　And slosh in the rain.
She loved to go out
　And get herself wet,
And she had a duck
　For her favourite pet.

Every day
　At half-past four
They'd both run out
　The kitchen door;
They'd find a puddle,
　And there they'd stay
Until it was time
　To go away.

They got quite wet,
　But they didn't mind;
And every rainy
　Day they'd find
A new way to splash
　Or a new way to swim.
And the duck loved Jane,
　And Jane loved him.

Marchette Chute

Careful Katie

Careful Katie cooked a crisp and crinkly cabbage;
Did careful Katie cook a crisp and crinkly cabbage?
If careful Katie cooked a crisp and crinkly cabbage,
Where's the crisp and crinkly cabbage careful Katie cooked?

Anon.

Inconsiderate Hannah

Naughty little Hannah said
   She could make her Grandma whistle;
So, that night, inside her bed
   Placed some nettles and a thistle.

Though dear Grandma quite infirm is,
   Heartless Hannah watched her settle
With her poor old epidermis
   Resting up against a nettle.

Suddenly she reached the thistle!
My! you should have heard her whistle!
. . . .
A successful plan was Hannah's,
But I cannot praise her manners.

D. Streamer

Maria Jane

It really gives me heartfelt pain
To tell you of Maria Jane,
For oh! she was so naughty!
Her nurse would weep and say: 'Ah me!
If you're so bad when only three,
What will you be at forty?'

She loved to paddle in the wet
'Till soaked with mud her clothes would get,
For oh! she was so dirty!
Her nurse would weep and cry: 'Ah me!
If you love dirt so much at three,
What will you love at thirty?'

Her appetite did all surprise,
Plum puddings, cakes and hot mince-pies,
For oh! she ne'er had plenty!
Her nurse would weep and scream: 'Ah me!
If you can eat so much at three,
What will you eat at twenty?'

Alfred Scott-Gatty

In the mirror

In the mirror
On the wall,
There's a face
I always see;
Round and pink,
And rather small,
Looking back again
At me.

It is very
Rude to stare,
But she never
Thinks of that,
For her eyes are
Always there;
What can she be
Looking at?

Elizabeth Fleming

Betty Botter

Betty Botter bought some butter,
But she said, 'My butter's bitter.
If I put it in my batter
It will make my batter bitter.
If I buy some better butter
It will make my batter better.'
So she bought some better butter
And it made her batter better.

Anon.

My sister Clarissa spits twice if I kiss her

My sister Clarissa spits twice if I kiss her
and once if I hold her hand.
I reprimand her – my name's Alexander –
for spitting I simply can't stand.

George Barker

Sink song

Scouring out the porridge pot,
   Round and round and round!

Out with all the scraith and scoopery.
Lift the eely ooly droopery,
Chase the glubbery slubbery gloopery
   Round and round and round!

Out with all the doleful dithery,
Ladle out the slimery slithery,
Hunt and catch the hithery thithery,
   Round and round and round!

Out with all the obbly gubbly,
On the stove it burns so bubbly,
Use the spoon and use it doubly,
   Round and round and round!

J. A. Lindon

Questions

(1)

If all the world were paper,
  If all the sea were ink,
If all the trees were bread and cheese,
  What would we have to drink?

If all the bottles leaked
  And none but had a crack,
If Spanish apes ate all the grapes,
  What would we do for sack?*

*Wine.

Anon.

(2)

The man in the wilderness asked of me
'How many strawberries grow in the sea?'
I answered him as I thought good,
'As many red herrings as grow in the wood.'

Anon.

(3)

I often wonder why, oh why,
All grown-ups say to me:
'When you are old and six foot high,
What do you want to be?'

I sometimes wonder what they'd say
If I should ask them all
What *they* would like to be, if they
Were six years old and small.

Raymond Wilson

(4)

If all the food was paving-stones,
And all the seas were ink,
What would we poor mortals do
For victuals and for drink?

Anon.

(5)

Ask no questions
And you'll be told no lies;
Shut your mouth
And you'll catch no flies.

Anon.

I went to Noke

I went to Noke,
But nobody spoke;
I went to Thame,
It was just the same;
Burford and Brill
Were silent and still;
But I went to Beckley
And they spoke directly.

Anon.

As I walked by myself

As I walked by myself,
And talked to myself,
   Myself said unto me,
'Look to thyself,
Take care of thyself,
   For nobody cares for thee.'

I answered myself,
And said to myself,
   In the self-same way to me,

'Look to thyself
Or not look to thyself,
   The self-same thing will be.'

Anon.

Topsy-Turvy Land

The people walk upon their heads,
The sea is made of sand,
The children go to school by night,
In Topsy-Turvy Land.

The front-door step is at the back,
You're walking when you stand,
You wear your hat upon your feet,
In Topsy-Turvy Land.

And buses on the sea you'll meet,
While pleasure boats are planned
To travel up and down the streets
Of Topsy-Turvy Land.

You pay for what you never get,
I think it must be grand,
For when you go you're coming back,
In Topsy-Turvy Land.

H. E. Wilkinson

The Land of the Bumbley Boo

In the Land of the Bumbley Boo
The people are red white and blue,
They never blow noses,
Or ever wear closes;
What a sensible thing to do!

In the Land of the Bumbley Boo
You can buy Lemon pie at the Zoo;
They give away Foxes
In little Pink Boxes
And Bottles of Dandelion Stew.

In the Land of the Bumbley Boo
You never see a Gnu,
But thousands of cats
Wearing trousers and hats
Made of Pumpkins and Pelican Glue!

Oh, the Bumbley Boo! the Bumbley Boo!
That's the place for me and you!
So hurry! Let's run!
The train leaves at one!
For the Land of the Bumbley Boo!
The wonderful Bumbley Boo-Boo-Boo!
The Wonderful Bumbley BOO!!!

Spike Milligan

'Twas midnight

'Twas midnight on the ocean,
Not a streetcar was in sight,
The sun was shining brightly,
For it rained all day that night.
'Twas a summer day in winter
And snow was raining fast
As a barefoot boy with shoes on
Stood sitting in the grass.

Anon.

One fine day

One fine day in the middle of the night
Two dead men got up to fight;
Two blind men to see fair play,
Two dumb men to shout: 'Hurray!'
And two lame men to carry them away.

Anon.

The moon

Not many cars about –
A jolly good place to play!
Not a window to break,
No tempers to fray.

The sixes I would knock!
If I hit a catch it would never land.
All day I could stand on my head,
The kids could play in the sand.

Those places up above,
They're made for bats and balls.
But what a long walk home
When supper calls.

D. J. Enright

The Man in the Moon

The Man in the Moon came tumbling down
   And asked the way to Norwich.
He went by the south and burnt his mouth
   With eating cold pease porridge.

Anon.

The animal fair

I went to the animal fair,
All the birds and the beasts were there.
The big baboon, by the light of the moon,
Was combing his auburn hair.
The monkey, he got drunk,
And sat on the elephant's trunk.
The elephant sneezed and fell on his knees,
And what became of the MONKEY,
                monkey,
                    monk?

                Anon.

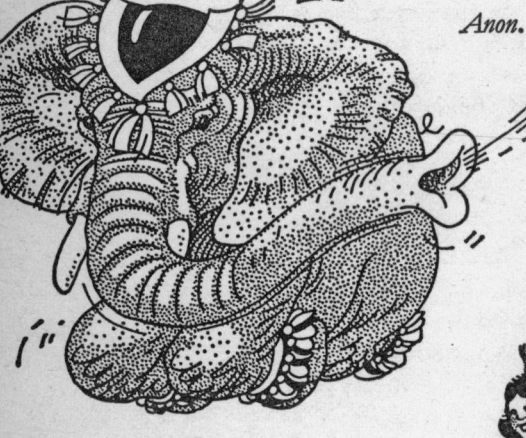

The roundabout

Round and round the roundabout,
Down the 'slippery stair' –
I'm always to be found about
When circus men are there.
The music of the roundabout,
The voices in the air,
The horses as they pound about,
The boys who shout and stare –
There's such a lovely sound about
A circus or a fair.

                Clive Sansom

Zoo manners

Be careful what
   You say or do
When you visit the animals
   At the Zoo.

Don't make fun
   Of the Camel's hump –
He's very proud
   Of his noble bump.

Don't laugh too much
   At the Chimpanzee –
He thinks he's as wise
   As you or me.

And the Penguins
   Strutting round the lake
Can understand
   Remarks you make.

Treat them as well
   As they do you,
And you'll always be welcome
   At the Zoo.

Eileen Mathias

The Rum Tum Tugger

The Rum Tum Tugger is a Curious Cat:
If you offer him pheasant he would rather have grouse.
If you put him in a house he would much prefer a flat,
If you put him in a flat then he'd rather have a house.
If you set him on a mouse then he only wants a rat,
If you set him on a rat then he'd rather chase a mouse.
Yes the Rum Tum Tugger is a Curious Cat —
    And there isn't any call for me to shout it:
      For he will do
      As he do do
         And there's no doing anything about it!

The Rum Tum Tugger is a terrible bore:
When you let him in, then he wants to be out;
He's always on the wrong side of every door,
And as soon as he's at home, then he'd like to get about.
He likes to lie in the bureau drawer,
But he makes such a fuss if he can't get out.
Yes the Rum Tum Tugger is a Curious Cat —
    And it isn't any use for you to doubt it:
      For he will do
      As he do do
         And there's no doing anything about it!

The Rum Tum Tugger is a curious beast:
His disobliging ways are a matter of habit.
If you offer him fish then he always wants a feast;
When there isn't any fish then he won't eat rabbit.
If you offer him cream then he sniffs and sneers,
For he only likes what he finds for himself;
So you'll catch him in it right up to the ears,
If you put it away on the larder shelf.
The Rum Tum Tugger is artful and knowing,
The Rum Tum Tugger doesn't care for a cuddle;
But he'll leap on your lap in the middle of your sewing,
For there's nothing he enjoys like a horrible muddle.
Yes the Rum Tum Tugger is a Curious Cat –
    And there isn't any need for me to spout it:
        For he will do
        As he do do
            And there's no doing anything about it!

T. S. Eliot

The owl and the pussy-cat

The Owl and the Pussy-cat went to sea
   In a beautiful pea-green boat,
They took some honey, and plenty of money,
   Wrapped up in a five-pound note.

The Owl looked up to the stars above,
   And sang to a small guitar,
'O lovely Pussy! O Pussy, my love,
   What a beautiful Pussy you are,
           You are,
           You are!
   What a beautiful Pussy you are!'

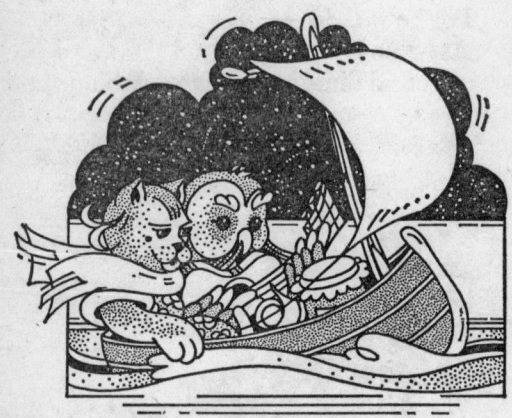

Pussy said to the Owl, 'You elegant fowl!
   How charmingly sweet you sing!
O let us be married! too long we have tarried!
   But what shall we do for a ring?'
They sailed away, for a year and a day,
   To the land where the Bong-tree grows,
And there in a wood a Piggy-wig stood,
   With a ring at the end of his nose,
           His nose,
           His nose,
   With a ring at the end of his nose.

'Dear Pig, are you willing to sell for one shilling
   Your ring?' Said the Piggy, 'I will.'
So they took it away, and were married next day
   By the Turkey who lives on the hill.
They dined on mince, and slices of quince,
   Which they ate with a runcible spoon;
And hand in hand, on the edge of the sand,
   They danced by the light of the moon,
         The moon,
         The moon,
   They danced by the light of the moon.

Edward Lear

I'm not frightened of pussy cats

I'm not frightened of Pussy Cats,
They only eat up mice and rats,
But a Hippopotamus
Could eat the Lotofus!

Spike Milligan

The song of the Jellicles

Jellicle Cats come out to-night,
Jellicle Cats come one come all:
The Jellicle Moon is shining bright –
Jellicles come to the Jellicle Ball.

Jellicle Cats are black and white,
Jellicle Cats are rather small;
Jellicle Cats are merry and bright,
And pleasant to hear when they caterwaul.
Jellicle Cats have cheerful faces,
Jellicle Cats have bright black eyes;
They like to practise their airs and graces
And wait for the Jellicle Moon to rise.

Jellicle Cats develop slowly,
Jellicle Cats are not too big;
Jellicle Cats are roly-poly,
They know how to dance a gavotte and a jig.
Until the Jellicle Moon appears
They make their toilette and take their repose:
Jellicles wash behind their ears,
Jellicles dry between their toes.

Jellicle Cats are white and black,
Jellicle Cats are of moderate size;
Jellicles jump like a jumping-jack,
Jellicle Cats have moonlit eyes.
They're quiet enough in the morning hours,
They're quiet enough in the afternoon,
Reserving their terpsichorean powers
To dance by the light of the Jellicle Moon.

Jellicle Cats are black and white,
Jellicle Cats (as I said) are small;
If it happens to be a stormy night
They will practise a caper or two in the hall.
If it happens the sun is shining bright
You would say they had nothing to do at all:
They are resting and saving themselves to be right
For the Jellicle Moon and the Jellicle Ball.

T. S. Eliot

Cat

My cat has got no name,
We simply call him Cat;
He doesn't seem to blame
Anyone for that.

For he is not like us
Who often, I'm afraid,
Kick up quite a fuss
If *our* names are mislaid.

As if, without a name,
We'd be no longer there
But like a tiny flame
Vanish in bright air.

My pet, he doesn't care
About such things as that:
Black buzz and golden stare
Require no name but Cat.

Vernon Scannell

Mice

I think mice
Are rather nice.

Their tails are long,
Their faces small,
They haven't any
Chins at all.
Their ears are pink,
Their teeth are white,
They run about
The house at night.
They nibble things
They shouldn't touch
And no one seems
To like them much.

But I think mice
Are nice.

Rose Fyleman

Stanley the rat

Stanley's a rat and a fast one at that,
From bulkhead to bulkhead in four seconds flat,
He's come and he's gone 'fore an eyelid can bat,
But he'd do it much quicker if we had a cat.

One flashing run and his visit is done,
Stan never lingers to join in the fun.
Our hospitality he'd rather shun,
But he'd stay a bit longer if we had a gun.

I raises my cap to this beady-eyed chap
Who needs no compass and carries no map,
And don't know what it means for to get in a flap,
But we'd bloomin' soon show him if we had a trap.

When does he doze? Nobody knows;
Night and day he keeps on his toes,
I don't suppose his eyes ever close,
But he'd sleep for ever and ever and ever
    if we had a high pressure hose.

Cyril Tawney

The two rats

He was a rat, and she was a rat,
    And down in one hole they did dwell;
And both were as black as a witch's cat,
    And they loved each other well.

He had a tail, and she had a tail,
    Both long, and curling, and fine;
And each said: 'Yours is the finest tail
    In the world, excepting mine.'

He smelt the cheese, and she smelt the cheese,
    And they both pronounced it good;
And both said it would greatly add
    To the charms of their daily food.

So he went out, and she went out,
    And I saw them go with pain;
And what befell them I never can tell,
    For they never came back again.

Anon.

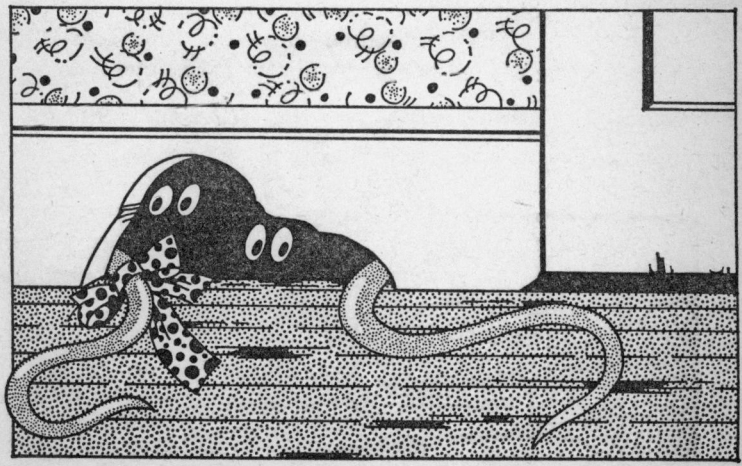

Skippets, the bad one

High upon the hillside where the shadows play
   Lives gentle Mrs Rabbit with her family of three,
And Spillikins and Spottikins, it's only right to say,
   Are the dearest little rabbits you can ever hope to see.
          But Skippets is the bad one,
            The mad one,
              The saucy one,
Skippets is the lazy one who won't wash his face.
          Skippets is the naughty one,
            The haughty one,
              The pushing one,
Skippets is the forward one who doesn't know his place.

Spillikins and Spottikins will never stay out late,
   And wander in the gloomy woods as many rabbits do.
Why, even in the summer-time, they're always in by eight –
   In case they catch a cold, you see, by sitting in the dew.

          But Skippets is the frisky one,
            The risky one,
              The roving one,
Skippets is the wilful one whose ways are hard to trace.
          Skippets is the careless one,
            The won't-come-home-at-bedtime one –
Skippets is the wicked one who's always in disgrace!

Christine E. Bradley

The clever rabbit

There was a little Rabbit
    who was lying in his burrow . . .
When the Dingo rang him up to say
    he'd call on him tomorrow . . .

But the Rabbit thought it better
    that the Dingo did not meet him;
So he found another burrow
    and the Dingo didn't eat him.

D. H. Souter

Grizzly bear

If you ever, ever, ever meet a grizzly bear,
You must never, never, never ask him *where*
He is going.
Or *what* he is doing;
For if you ever, ever, dare
To stop a grizzly bear,
You will never meet *another* grizzly bear.

Mary Austin

Algy

Algy saw a bear;
The bear saw Algy.
The bear had a bulge;
The bulge was Algy.
        Anon.

The grizzly bear

The Grizzly Bear is huge and wild;
He has devoured the infant child.
The infant child is not aware
He has been eaten by the bear.

Alfred Edward Housman

Teddy Bear

Teddy Bear
Sat on a chair,
With ham and jam
And plum and pear.

'This is queer,'
Said Teddy Bear,
'The more I eat
The less is there!'

L. H. Allen

The six badgers

As I was a-hoeing, a-hoeing my lands
Six badgers came up with white wands in their hands.
They made a ring around me and, bowing, they said:
'Hurry home, Farmer George, for the table is spread!
There's pie in the oven, there's beef on the plate:
Hurry home, Farmer George, if you would not be late!'
So homeward I went, but could not understand
Why six fine dog-badgers with white wands in hand
Should seek me out hoeing and bow in a ring,
And all to inform me so common a thing!

Robert Graves

Derby ram

As I was going to Derby, Sir, 'twas on a summer's day,
I met the finest ram, Sir, that ever was fed on hay,
And indeed, Sir, 'tis true, Sir, I never was given to lie,
And if you'd been to Derby, Sir, you'd have seen him as well as I.

It had four feet to walk on, Sir, it had four feet to stand,
And every foot it had, Sir, did cover an acre of land.
And indeed, Sir, 'tis true, Sir, I never was given to lie,
And if you'd been to Derby, Sir, you'd have seen him as well as I.

This ram it had a horn, Sir, that reached up to the sky,
The birds went up and built their nests, could hear the
   young ones cry.
And indeed, Sir, 'tis true, Sir, I was never given to lie,
And if you'd been to Derby, Sir, you'd have seen him as well as I.

This ram he had another horn that reached up to the moon,
The birds went up in January and didn't come down till June.
And indeed, Sir, 'tis true, Sir, I never was given to lie,
And if you'd been to Derby, Sir, you'd have seen him as well as I.

And all the men of Derby, Sir, came begging for his tail
To ring St George's passing-bell at the top of Derby jail.
And indeed, Sir, 'tis true, Sir, I never was given to lie,
And if you'd been to Derby, Sir, you'd have seen him as well as I.

And all the women of Derby, Sir, came begging for his ears
To make them leather aprons to last them forty years.
And indeed, Sir, 'tis true, Sir, I never was given to lie,
And if you'd been to Derby, Sir, you'd have seen him as well as I.

And all the boys of Derby, Sir, came begging for his eyes
To make a pair of footballs, for they were just the size.
And indeed, Sir, 'tis true, Sir, I never was given to lie,
And if you'd been to Derby, Sir, you'd have seen him as well as I.

The butcher that killed this ram, Sir, was in danger of his life,
He was up to his knees in blood crying out for a longer knife.
And indeed, Sir, 'tis true, Sir, I never was given to lie,
And if you'd been to Derby, Sir, you'd have seen him as well as I.

And now my song is ended, I have no more to say,
So please will you give us a New Year's gift, and let us go away.
And indeed, Sir, 'tis true, Sir, I never was given to lie,
And if you'd been to Derby, Sir, you'd have seen him as well as I.

Anon.

As I went to Bonner

As I went to Bonner,
    I met a pig
    Without a wig,
Upon my word and honour.

Anon.

The lady and the swine

There was a lady loved a swine.
    'Honey,' said she,
'Pig-hog, wilt thou be mine?'
    'Hunc,' said he.

'I'll build for thee a silver sty,
    Honey,' said she,
'And in it softly thou shalt lie.'
    'Hunc,' said he.

Anon.

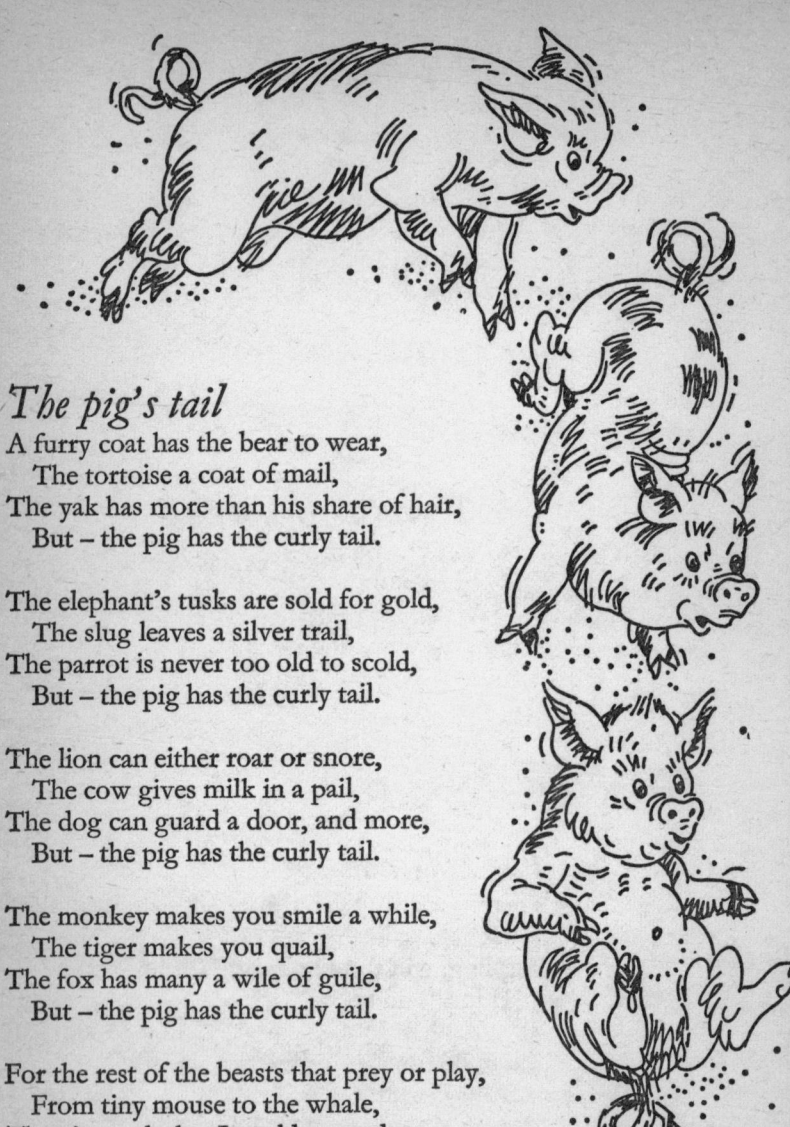

The pig's tail

A furry coat has the bear to wear,
　　The tortoise a coat of mail,
The yak has more than his share of hair,
　　But – the pig has the curly tail.

The elephant's tusks are sold for gold,
　　The slug leaves a silver trail,
The parrot is never too old to scold,
　　But – the pig has the curly tail.

The lion can either roar or snore,
　　The cow gives milk in a pail,
The dog can guard a door, and more,
　　But – the pig has the curly tail.

The monkey makes you smile a while,
　　The tiger makes you quail,
The fox has many a wile of guile,
　　But – the pig has the curly tail.

For the rest of the beasts that prey or play,
　　From tiny mouse to the whale,
There's much that I could say today,
　　But – the pig has the curly tail.

Norman Ault

The tale of a dog and a bee

Great big dog,
  Head upon his toes;
Tiny little bee
  Settles on his nose.

Great big dog
  Thinks it is a fly.
Never says a word,
  Winks very sly.

Tiny little bee,
  Tickles dog's nose –
Thinks like as not
  'Tis a pretty rose.

Dog smiles a smile,
  Winks his other eye,
Chuckles to himself
  How he'll catch a fly.

Then he makes a snap,
  Very quick and spry,
Does his level best,
  But doesn't catch the fly.

Tiny little bee,
  Alive and looking well;
Great big dog,
  Mostly gone to swell.

MORAL:
Dear friends and brothers all,
  Don't be too fast and free,
And when you catch a fly,
  Be sure it's not a bee.

Anon.

Cows

Half the time they munched the grass,
    and all the time they lay
Down in the water-meadows, the lazy month
    of May,
        A-chewing,
        A-mooing,
     To pass the time away.
     Nice weather,
              said the brown cow.
    Ah,
      said the white.
    Grass is very tasty.
    Grass is all right.

Half the time they munched the grass,
    and all the time they lay
Down in the water-meadows, the lazy month
    of May,
        A-chewing,
        A-mooing,
     To pass the time away.
     Rain coming,
              said the brown cow.
    Ah,
      said the white.
    Flies is very tiresome.
    Flies bite.

Half the time they munched the grass,
    and all the time they lay
Down in the water-meadows, the lazy month
    of May,
        A-chewing,
        A-mooing,
      To pass the time away.
      Time to go,
               said the brown cow.
      Ah,
        said the white.
      Nice chat.
      Very pleasant.
      Night.
      Night.

Half the time they munched the grass,
    and half the time they lay
Down in the water-meadows, the lazy month
    of May,
        A-chewing,
        A-mooing,
      To pass the time away.

James Reeves

The cow

I'm very sorry for
A cow;
Its clothes seem fashioned
Anyhow;
They never look as if they
Fit;
I wonder what is wrong
With it?

And if a cow should need
A patch
It never chooses one
To match,
But makes the oddest pieces
Do.

I think it's rather sad;
Don't you?

Elizabeth Fleming

The cow

The cow stood on the hillside,
Its skin as smooth as silk,
It slipped upon a cowslip,
And sprained a pint of milk.

Anon.

I never saw a purple cow

I never saw a Purple Cow,
  I never hope to see one;
But I can tell you, anyhow,
  I'd rather see than be one!

Gelett Burgess

The plaint of the camel

Canary-birds feed on sugar and seed,
  Parrots have crackers to crunch;
And as for the poodles, they tell me the noodles
  Have chicken and cream for their lunch.
But there's never a question
About MY digestion,
  ANYTHING does for me.

Cats, you're aware, can repose in a chair,
  Chickens can roost upon rails;
Puppies are able to sleep in a stable,
  And oysters can slumber in pails.
But no one supposes
A poor Camel dozes.
  ANY PLACE does for me.

Lambs are enclosed where it's never exposed,
  Coops are constructed for hens;
Kittens are treated to houses well heated,
  And pigs are protected by pens.
But a Camel comes handy
Wherever it's sandy,
  ANYWHERE does for me.

People would laugh if you rode a giraffe,
  Or mounted the back of an ox;
It's nobody's habit to ride on a rabbit,
  Or try to bestraddle a fox.
But as for a Camel, he's
Ridden by families –
  ANY LOAD does for me.

A snake is as round as a hole in the ground;
  Weasels are wavy and sleek;
And no alligator could ever be straighter
  Than lizards that live in a creek.
But a camel's all lumpy,
And bumpy and humpy
  ANY SHAPE does for me.

Charles Edward Carryl

How doth the little crocodile

How doth the little crocodile
  Improve his shining tail,
And pour the waters of the Nile
  On every golden scale!

How cheerfully he seems to grin,
  How neatly spreads his claws,
And welcomes little fishes in,
  With gently smiling jaws!

Lewis Carroll

If you should meet a crocodile

If you should meet a crocodile,
    Don't take a stick and poke him;
Ignore the welcome in his smile,
    Be careful not to stroke him.

For as he sleeps upon the Nile,
    He thinner gets and thinner;
And whene'er you meet a crocodile
    He's ready for his dinner.

Anon.

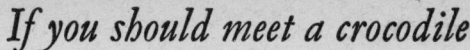

S–JJ–D

The frog

What a wonderful bird the frog are –
When he sit, he stand almost;
When he hop, he fly almost.
He ain't got no sense hardly;
He ain't got no tail hardly either.
When he sit, he sit on what he ain't got – almost.

Anon.

St Jerome and his lion

St Jerome in his study kept a great big cat,
It's always in his pictures, with its feet upon the mat.
Did he give it milk to drink, in a little dish?
When it came to Fridays, did he give it fish?
If I lost my little cat, I'd be sad without it;
I should ask St Jeremy what to do about it;
I should ask St Jeremy, just because of that,
For he's the only saint I know who kept a pussy cat.

Anon.

The kangaroo

Old Jumpety-Bumpety-Hop-and-Go-One
Was lying asleep on his side in the sun.
This old kangaroo, he was whisking the flies
(With his long glossy tail) from his ears and his eyes.
Jumpety-Bumpety-Hop-and-Go-One
Was lying asleep on his side in the sun,
Jumpety-Bumpety-Hop!

Anon.

Habits of the hippopotamus

The hippopotamus is strong
And huge of head and broad of bustle;
The limbs on which he rolls along
Are big with hippopotomuscle.

He does not greatly care for sweets
Like ice-cream, apple pie, or custard,
But takes to flavour what he eats
A little hippopotomustard.

The hippopotamus is true
To all his principles, and just;
He always tries his best to do
The things one hippopotomust.

He never rides in trucks or trams,
In taxicabs or omnibuses,
And so keeps out of traffic jams
And other hippopotomusses.

Arthur Guiterman

The big baboon

The Big Baboon is found upon
   The plains of Cariboo:
He goes about with nothing on
   (A shocking thing to do).

But if he dressed respectably
   And let his whiskers grow,
How like this Big Baboon would be
   To Mister So-and-so!

Hilaire Belloc

The elephant knocked the ground

The elephant knocked the ground with a stick,
He knocked it slow, he knocked it quick.
He knocked it till his trunk turned black –
Then the ground turned round and knocked him back.

Adrian Mitchell

Calico Pie

Calico Pie,
The little Birds fly
Down to the calico tree,
Their wings were blue,
And they sang 'Tilly-loo!'
Till away they flew, –
And they never came back to me!
They never came back!
They never came back!
They never came back to me!

Calico Jam,
The little Fish swam,
Over the syllabub sea,
He took off his hat,
To the Sole and the Sprat,
And the Willeby-wat, –
But he never came back to me!
He never came back!
He never came back!
He never came back to me!

Calico Ban,
The little Mice ran,
To be ready in time for tea,
Flippity flup,
They drank it all up,
And danced in the cup, –
But they never came back to me!
They never came back!
They never came back!
They never came back to me!

Calico Drum,
The Grasshoppers come,
The Butterfly, Beetle, and Bee,
Over the ground,
Around and round,
With a hop and a bound, –
But they never came back!
They never came back!
They never came back!
They never came back to me!

Edward Lear

The tale of Custard the dragon

Belinda lived in a little white house,
With a little black kitten and a little grey mouse,
And a little yellow dog and a little red wagon,
And a realio, trulio, little pet dragon.

Now the name of the little black kitten was Ink,
And the little grey mouse, she called her Blink,
And the little yellow dog was sharp as Mustard,
But the dragon was a coward, and she called him Custard.

Custard the dragon had big sharp teeth,
And spikes on top of him and scales underneath,
Mouth like a fireplace, chimney for a nose,
And realio, trulio, daggers on his toes.

Belinda was as brave as a barrelful of bears,
And Ink and Blink chased lions down the stairs,
Mustard was as brave as a tiger in a rage,
But Custard cried for a nice safe cage.

Belinda tickled him, she tickled him unmerciful,
Ink, Blink and Mustard, they rudely called him Percival,
They all sat laughing in the little red wagon
At the realio, trulio, cowardly dragon.

Belinda giggled till she shook the house,
And Blink said *Weeek!*, which is giggling for a mouse,
Ink and Mustard rudely asked his age,
When Custard cried for a nice safe cage.

Suddenly, suddenly they heard a nasty sound,
And Mustard growled, and they all looked around.
Meowch! cried Ink, and Ooh! cried Belinda,
For there was a pirate, climbing in the winda.

Pistol in his left hand, pistol in his right,
And he held in his teeth a cutlass bright;
His beard was black, one leg was wood.
It was clear that the pirate meant no good.

Belinda paled, and she cried Help! Help!
But Mustard fled with a terrified yelp,
Ink trickled down to the bottom of the household,
And little mouse Blink strategically mouseholed.

But up jumped Custard, snorting like an engine,
Clashed his tail like irons in a dungeon,
With a clatter and a clank and a jangling squirm
He went at the pirate like a robin at a worm.

The pirate gaped at Belinda's dragon,
And gulped some grog from his pocket flagon,
He fired two bullets, but they didn't hit,
And Custard gobbled him, every bit.

Belinda embraced him, Mustard licked him;
No one mourned for his pirate victim.
Ink and Blink in glee did gyrate
Around the dragon that ate the pyrate.

Belinda still lives in her little white house,
With her little black kitten and her little grey mouse,
And her little yellow dog and her little red wagon,
And her realio, trulio, little pet dragon.

Belinda is as brave as a barrelful of bears,
And Ink and Blink chase lions down the stairs,
Mustard is as brave as a tiger in a rage,
But Custard keeps crying for a nice safe cage.

Ogden Nash

The Bongaloo

'What is a Bongaloo, Daddy?'
'A Bongaloo, Son,' said I,
'Is a tall bag of cheese
Plus a Chinaman's knees
And the leg of a nanny goat's eye.'

'How strange is a Bongaloo, Daddy?'
'As strange as strange,' I replied.
'When the sun's in the West
It appears in a vest
Sailing out with the noonday tide.'

'What shape is a Bongaloo, Daddy?'
'The shape, my Son, I'll explain:
It's tall round the nose
Which continually grows
In the general direction of Spain.'

'Are you *sure* there's a Bongaloo, Daddy?'
'Am I sure, my Son?' said I.
'Why, I've seen it, not quite
On a dark sunny night
Do you think that I'd tell you a lie?'

Spike Milligan

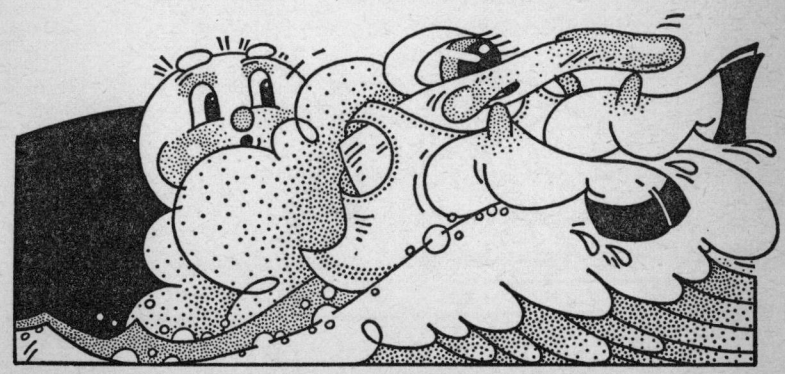

The Bogus-boo

The Bogus-boo
Is a creature who
Comes out at night—and why?
He likes the air;
He likes to scare
The nervous passer-by.

Out from the park
At dead of dark
He comes with huffling pad.
If, when alone,
You hear his moan,
'Tis like to drive you mad.

He has two wings,
Pathetic things,
With which he cannot fly.
His tusks look fierce,
Yet could not pierce
The merest butterfly.

He has six ears,
But what he hears
Is very faint and small;
And with the claws
On his eight paws
He cannot scratch at all.

He looks so wise
With his owl-eyes,
His aspect grim and ghoulish;
But truth to tell,
He sees not well
And is distinctly foolish.

This Bogus-boo,
What can he do
But huffle in the dark?
So don't take fright;
He has no bite
And very little bark.

James Reeves

The horny-goloch

The horny-goloch is an awesome beast,
Supple an' scaly;
It has twa horns, an' a hantle* o' feet
An' a forkie tailie.

* lots

Anon.

Whale

Wouldn't you like to be a whale
And sail serenely by –
An eighty-foot whale from the tip of your tail
And a tiny briny eye?
Wouldn't you like to wallow
Where nobody says 'Come out!'?
Wouldn't you *love* to swallow
And blow all the brine about?
Wouldn't you like to be always clean
But never to have to wash, I mean,
And wouldn't you love to spout –
  O yes, just think –
A feather of spray as you sail away,
And rise and sink and rise and sink,
And blow all the brine about?

Geoffrey Dearmer

Alas!

Ann, Ann!
Come! quick as you can!
There's a fish that talks
In the frying-pan.
Out of the fat,
As clear as glass,
He put up his mouth
And moaned 'Alas!'
Oh, most mournful,
'Alas, alack!'
Then turned to his sizzling,
And sank him back.

Anon.

Goldfish

One small fish in a
Polythene bag;
Can't swim round, can
Only look sad.
Take a pair of scissors,
Snip a quick hole,
Down flops water
And fish into a bowl!

She waits a little moment,
Flips her tail free,
Then off into circles
As frisk as can be.
Dash-about – splash-about –
Do what you wish;
You're mine, you black-spotted
Cheeky-eyed
Fish!

John Walsh

Quack

The duck is whiter than whey is,
His tail tips up over his back,
The eye in his head is as round as a button,
And he says, *Quack! Quack!*

He swims on his bright blue mill-pond,
By the willow-tree under the shack,
Then stands on his head to see down to the bottom,
And says, *Quack! Quack!*

When Molly steps out of the kitchen,
For apron – pinned round with a sack –
He squints at her round face, her dish, and what's in it,
And says, *Quack! Quack!*

He preens the pure snow of his feathers
In the sun by the wheat-straw stack;
At dusk waddles home with his brothers and sisters,
And says, *Quack! Quack!*

Walter de la Mare

The reason for the pelican

The reason for the pelican
Is difficult to see:
His beak is clearly larger
Than there's any need to be.

It's not to bail a boat with –
He doesn't own a boat.
Yet everywhere he takes himself
He has that beak to tote.

It's not to keep his wife in –
His wife has got one, too.
It's not a scoop for eating soup.
It's not an extra shoe.

It isn't quite for anything.
And yet you realise
It's really quite a splendid beak
In quite a splendid size.

John Ciardi

Toucannery

whatever one toucan can do
is sooner done by toucans two
and three toucans it's very true
can do much more than two can do

and toucans numbering two plus two can
manage more than all the zoo can
in fact there is no toucan who can
do what four or three or two can.

Jack Prelutsky

The common cormorant

The common cormorant (or shag)
Lays eggs inside a paper bag,
You follow the idea, no doubt?
It's to keep the lightning out.

But what these unobservant birds
Have never thought of, is that herds
Of wandering bears might come with buns
And steal the bags to hold the crumbs.

Anon.

Ploffskin, pluffskin

Ploffskin, pluffskin, Pelican jee!
We think no birds so happy as we!
Plumpkin, Ploshkin, Pelican jill!
We think so then, and we thought so still!

Edward Lear

Three little puffins

Three little puffins
Were partial to muffins,
As partial as partial can be.
They wouldn't eat nuffin'
But hot buttered muffin
For breakfast and dinner and tea.
Pantin' and puffin'
And chewin' and chuffin'
They just went on stuffin', dear me!
Till the three little puffins
Were chockful of muffins
And puffy as puffy can be,
All three
Were puffy as puffy can be.

Eleanor Farjeon

A little cock sparrow

A little cock sparrow sat on a tree,
Looking as happy as happy could be,
Till a boy came by with his bow and arrow:
Says he, 'I'll shoot that little cock sparrow.

His body will make a nice little stew,
And perhaps there'll be some for a little pie too.'
Says the little cock sparrow, 'I'll be shot if I stay,'
So he flapped his wings and flew away!

Anon.

Two sparrows

Two sparrows, feeding,
heard a thrush
sing to the dawn,
the first said, 'Tush!

in all my life
I never heard
a more affected
singing bird.'

The second said,
'It's you and me,
who slave to keep
the likes of he.'

'And if we cared,'
both sparrows said,
'we'd do that singing
on our head.'

The thrush pecked sideways
and was dumb.
'And now,' they screamed,
'he's pinched our crumb.'

Humbert Wolfe

Wise bird

A very wise bird with a very long beak
  Sat solemnly blinking away.
When asked why it was that he never would speak,
  He replied: 'I have nothing to say.'

Anon.

My dame hath a lame tame crane

My dame hath a lame tame crane,
My dame hath a crane that is lame.
Pray, gentle Jane,
Let my dame's lame tame crane
Feed and come home again.

Anon.

Riddle-me-ree

(1)

There is one that has a head without an eye,
    And there's one that has an eye without a head:
You may find the answer if you try;
    And when all is said,
Half the answer hangs upon a thread.

Christina Rossetti

(2)

In Spring I look gay
Deck'd in comely array,
In Summer more clothing I wear;
    When colder it grows
    I fling off my clothes,
And in Winter quite naked appear.

Anon.

(3)

Voiceless it cries,
Wingless flutters,
Toothless bites,
Mouthless mutters.

J. R. R. Tolkien

(4)

I have no voice and yet I speak to you,
I tell of all things in the world that people do;
I have leaves, but I am not a tree,
I have pages, but I am not a bride or royalty;
I have a spine and hinges, but I am not a man or a door,
I have told you all . . . I cannot tell you more.

John Cuncliffe

(*For the answers turn to page 126.*)

Rest in Peace

(1)

He passed the bobby without any fuss,
And he passed the cart of hay,
He tried to pass a swerving bus,
And then he passed away.

Anon.

(2)

Here lies the body of Michael Shay
Who died maintaining his right of way.
His case was clear and his will was strong –
But he's as dead as if he'd been wrong.

Anon.

(3)

Here lies the body of Elizabeth White;
She signalled left, but turned to the right.

Anon.

(4)

Beyond these gates
Tom Green's at rest;
He took off his plates
But hadn't passed his test.

Anon.

(5)

Beneath this stone, a lump of clay,
Lies Uncle Peter Dan'els,
Who, early in the month of May,
Took off his winter flannels.

Anon.

Black is the raven,
Black is the rook;
But blacker the sinner
Who pinches this book.

Anon.

Index of first lines

Answers to Riddle-me-ree *(page 118)*

(1)   A pin and a needle.
(2)   A tree.
(3)   The wind.
(4)   A book.

More Beaver Books

We hope you have enjoyed this Beaver Book. Here are some of the other titles:

Time's Delights A Beaver original. A collection of poems old and new about all aspects of time, chosen by Raymond Wilson, with enchanting illustrations by Meg Rutherford

Rhyme Time A Beaver original. Over 200 poems specially chosen by Barbara Ireson to introduce younger readers to the pleasures of reading verse. This lively collection is illustrated throughout by Lesley Smith

The Tail of the Trinosaur Charles Causley's splendidly funny verse story about a prehistoric beast which comes to England from the Amazon jungle; with illustrations by Jill Gardiner

Pigeons and Princesses Five tales set in the world of legend and magic; James Reeves' lively prose is well matched by Edward Ardizzone's nostalgic illustrations

Covens and Cauldrons An anthology of stories, folk tales, poems and legends about witches, edited by Jacynth Hope-Simpson and strikingly illustrated by Krystyna Turska

New Beavers are published every month and if you would like the *Beaver Bulletin* – which gives all the details – please send a large stamped addressed envelope to:

Beaver Bulletin
The Hamlyn Group
Astronaut House
Feltham
Middlesex TW14 9AR

391612